NUMBERS
ALL AROUND

Susan Canizares • Betsey Chessen

Scholastic Inc.

New York • Toronto • London • Auckland • Sydney

Acknowledgments

Literacy Specialist: Linda Cornwell

Early Childhood Consultant: Ellen Booth Church

Design: Silver Editions

Photo Research: Silver Editions

Endnotes: Susan Russell

Endnote Illustrations: Ruth Flanigan

Photographs: Cover: Jan Halaska/Photo Researchers, Inc.; p. 1: Susan van Etten/Photo Edit; p. 2: David Young-Wolff/Photo Edit; p. 3: David Madison/Tony Stone Images; p. 4: Alan Hicks/Tony Stone Images; p. 5: Spencer Grant/Photo Researchers, Inc.; p. 6: Henley & Savage/The Stock Market; p. 7: Jack Reznicki/The Stock Market; p. 8: Michael Newman/Photo Edit; p. 9: M. Mastrorillo/The Stock Market; p. 10: Alan Wycheck/Gamma Liaison; p. 11: Jan Halaska/Photo Researchers, Inc.; p. 12: Stephen Saks/Photo Researchers, Inc.

Library of Congress Cataloging-in-Publication Data
Canizares, Susan 1960-
Numbers all around/Susan Canizares, Betsey Chessen.
p.cm. -- (Learning centers emergent readers)
Summary: Simple text and photographs
depict the numbers one to twelve in interesting places.
ISBN 0-439-04598-3 (pbk.: alk. paper)
1. Counting--Juvenile literature. [1. Counting.]
I. Chessen, Betsey, 1970-. II. Title. III. Series.
QA113.C36 1998

513.2'11--dc21

98-54205
CIP AC

28 27 26 25 24 23 22 21 20 19   08   10 11 12 13 14 15/0

one

two

three

four

five

six

seven

eight

nine

ten

eleven

twelve

NUMBERS ALL AROUND

If you look around, you'll see numbers all over the place. Numbers give us directions when we want to go somewhere, help us count things, help us measure things, and tell us how much something costs. There are numbers on signs, buildings, clocks, money, clothing, calendars, houses, and telephones. Numbers are everywhere.

One When there are many fire engines that look exactly alike, giving each one a number lets you know just which one is which. This picture shows fire engine Number 1. This fire engine has a special place at the firehouse and a particular team of firefighters who work with it. Its number tells the firefighters which engine is theirs.

Two Some things, like pencils, have numbers so that you'll know what's inside. The outside of many things is the same but the inside is different. Numbers can tell you the difference. The lead of number 2 pencils is softer than the lead of number 3 pencils and they make darker lines. The lead of number 1 pencils is softest and makes the darkest lines.

Three When you are watching a game from far away in the stands or on television, it's hard to tell which player is which. The large numbers on the uniforms help you tell the players apart. Most players wear numbers, not names.

Four At rodeos, numbers identify places. The place where the horse comes out is called a chute. The people who are watching the event can look at a particular chute number to find the next rider or to see a championship horse that's being announced.

Five Numbers help workers identify their equipment. In a fire station, many boots and helmets that look just alike are lined up all in a row. When there's a fire, each firefighter can quickly find his own equipment because it has a number on it. Numbers help with that quick identification and are very important in a firefighter's job.

Six Numbers are often the names of streets. In many towns and cities, numbers name many of the streets. And that often gives you extra information. If you happen to be on 6th Street, for instance, you'll know that 7th Street is the next one!

Seven Numbers also can tell you about time. This sign shows you that the hardware store is open every day. Numbers also tell you about opening and closing times. Most businesses put a sign with this information in the front window.

Eight It can be very difficult to tell one schoolbus from another. They all look very much alike. Numbers tell you one from another. This is very important information when buses that look just alike are taking different routes. These children know where the number 8 bus is going!

Nine Believe it or not, this huge number 9 sits right in the middle of the sidewalk! It is in New York City and tells us the address of the building behind it. Most addresses are printed on the buildings themselves, and are not nearly so big. The designers of this building turned the address number into a sidewalk sculpture. It certainly makes the building easy to find!

Ten The paper money that we use in the United States is all the exact same size and color. The easiest way to tell the difference is to look for the number. This 10-dollar bill equals the same amount of money as 10 bills that have number 1 printed on them! It's also worth the same as 2 bills with the number 5. When you buy something, look at the numbers on the bills to make sure you're getting the right change!

Eleven These houses are very colorful, but they also look very much alike. Addresses use numbers. They are on houses, apartments, and mailboxes. They help us find the place we're looking for. Numbers also help postal carriers deliver the right mail. It's important that you know the numbers in your address.

Twelve If you don't know the number of the train to get on, you might find yourself going to the wrong place! Numbers let us know which trains are going to which destinations. Like many public vehicles, trains have numbers to identify each one.